DEBT DOESN'T DISAPPEAR

Face it, Fix it, and finally Break Free

Simone Graham

Portions of this book were structured and refined with the assistance of AI technology to enhance clarity, organization, and accessibility while maintaining the author's original insights and expertise.

For permissions or enquiries, please contact:
contact@simones-solutions.com

Disclaimer:

The information provided in this book is for educational and informational purposes only and is based on personal experiences, research, and general financial principles. I am not a financial advisor, and this book does not constitute professional financial advice. Every financial situation is unique, and readers are encouraged to seek guidance from a qualified financial professional before making any major financial decisions. The strategies and tips shared are intended to help you improve your financial awareness and habits, but results may vary based on individual circumstances.

Contents

INTRODUCTION: WHY YOU NEED THIS BOOK

I know what it's like.... you feel your money disappears before the month is even over. I've been there, checking my bank account and wondering where it all went, dreading bills, and feeling stuck in a cycle of debt. The stress of financial struggle doesn't just sit in your bank account, it seeps into every part of your life. It affects your mental health, your relationships, and even your self-esteem.

But here's what changed everything for me, *I took control of my finances instead of letting my finances control me.*

No I didn't suddenly start earning six figures overnight. I didn't win the lottery. What I did was learn how to manage my money, understand my financial behaviours, and use simple strategies to break free from debt and start saving—without giving up the things I enjoy in life.

This book will guide you through that exact transformation. It's not about depriving yourself or following complicated finance jargon. It's about understanding your money, creating a plan that works for you, and making steady progress toward financial security.

And don't worry—you won't be doing this alone. That's why I created the **Break Free Budget Tracker**, which covers up to 5 years of creating financial stability for yourself, a personal tool to help you manage your income, expenses, debt, and savings. We'll be referring to it throughout the book, and by the time you're done, you'll know exactly how to use it to take control of your money.

If you've ever thought:

❌ "I can't save because I don't earn enough."
❌ "I'll never be debt-free."
❌ "I'm just bad with money."

Then this book is for you. Let's rewrite your financial story together.

Transform Your Mindset to Elevate Your Life: The Power of Neuroplasticity

Your brain is not fixed—it has the ability to change and adapt, no matter your age or financial situation. This is thanks to neuroplasticity, which is your brain's way of forming new connections and habits over time.

If you've always struggled with money, whether it's overspending, avoiding financial responsibilities, or believing you'll never be financially stable, it's not because you're "bad with money." It's simply because your brain has been wired to follow certain patterns. The good news? You can rewire it.

By consistently practicing new financial habits, such as budgeting, saving, or thinking positively about money, your brain will start to build stronger connections around these behaviours, making them feel more natural over time. The key is repetition and consistency. Just like learning a new skill, the more you practice, the easier it becomes.

However, it's not just about changing your habits, it's also about changing your environment. The people around you, the conversations you engage in, and the habits of those closest to you all influence your financial mindset. If you're trying to break free from a cycle of poor financial decisions, but you're surrounded by people who encourage overspending or have a negative attitude toward money, this will create resistance to your progress.

To truly transform your financial future, you need to be mindful of your surroundings. That doesn't mean cutting people off, but it does mean setting boundaries, seeking out financially responsible influences, and making conscious choices about who and what you allow to shape your mindset. When you align both your habits and your environment with your financial goals, you set yourself up for long-term success.

FINANCIAL TERMINOLOGY MADE SIMPLE

Dealing with debt and financial hardship can feel overwhelming, especially when you're faced with confusing financial jargon. Creditors, banks, and financial institutions often use terms that make things seem more complicated than they really are.

Before we dive into the strategies and creditor letters that will help you take control of your finances, let's breakdown some of the key terms you'll come across. This will help you feel more confident when negotiating, making financial decisions.

Use this section as a quick reference whenever you need clarity, it's here to empower you, not confuse you. Let's make financial language simple and easy to understand.

1. Creditor

A person or company you owe money to—like a bank, credit card company, or loan provider.

2. Debtor

That's you! A debtor is anyone who owes money to a creditor.

3. Interest

The extra cost you pay for borrowing money, usually a percentage of your balance. High interest means you pay more over time.

4. APR (Annual Percentage Rate)

The total yearly cost of borrowing, including interest and fees. A higher APR means a more expensive loan or credit card.

5. Minimum Payment

The smallest amount you must pay on a debt each month to avoid late fees—but paying only the minimum keeps you in debt longer.

6. Default

When you fail to pay a debt for a certain period, usually leading to penalties, a damaged credit score, or legal action.

7. CCJ (County Court Judgment)

A legal order issued if you fail to repay debt in the UK. This can affect your ability to borrow money in the future.

8. IVA (Individual Voluntary Arrangement)

A formal debt repayment plan in the UK where you agree to pay back a portion of your debt over time, helping avoid bankruptcy.

9. Bankruptcy

A legal process that writes off most of your debts if you can't afford to pay them, but it has long-term consequences for your credit.

10. Debt Management Plan (DMP)

An informal agreement where a third party negotiates with creditors to set up lower, more manageable payments.

11. Consolidation Loan

A loan that combines multiple debts into one, ideally with a lower interest rate to make repayment easier.

12. Secured vs. Unsecured Debt

- **Secured Debt** – Backed by an asset (like a mortgage on a house). If you don't pay, the lender can take the asset.
- **Unsecured Debt** – Not tied to any asset (like credit cards or personal loans).

13. Freeze on Interest & Charges

When a creditor agrees to stop adding interest or fees to help you catch up on payments.

14. Write-Off

When a creditor agrees to cancel your debt, usually if you prove you can't afford to pay.

15. Statute-Barred Debt

A debt that is so old (typically six years in the UK) that creditors can no longer take legal action to collect it.

By understanding these terms, you'll feel more in control when dealing with creditors, payment plans, and financial institutions. Knowledge is power—the more you know, the stronger your financial position becomes.

CHAPTER 1:
THE PSYCHOLOGY OF MONEY

Understanding Your Relationship with Money

Before we dive into numbers, budgets, and debt strategies, we need to talk about something deeper.....your relationship with money. Because money isn't just about math; it's about emotions, habits, and mindset.

Why Do We Spend the Way We Do?

Most of our financial behaviours are shaped by our past experiences. Think back to your childhood, how was money talked about (or not talked about) in your home?

Personal Story:

Growing up, I saw my parents worked hard to get the thing they wanted in life, money was something to be protected, I learned that money was for survival, not to be wasted on things that didn't add value and spent on the best deals. So when I started making my own money, I did what a lot of people do, I spent it as soon as I got it. Because deep down, I believed that money wasn't something you could hold onto for long and should be enjoyed. After all I worked hard for it......right?

Maybe your experience was different. Maybe you grew up in a household where money wasn't discussed at all, and now you feel lost when it comes to managing it. Or maybe money was seen as a status symbol, and now you feel pressure to always "keep up."

Whatever your background, your relationship with money was shaped by something. And until we identify and understand those patterns, it's hard to break free from them.

Common Money Mindsets (And How to Change Them)

1. The Scarcity Mindset

- Thought pattern: "There's never enough money."
- Behaviour: Constant stress about money, hoarding it, or avoiding financial decisions altogether.
- Fix: Shift to an abundance mindset by tracking what you DO have and creating a plan to grow it.

2. The "I Deserve This" Mindset

- Thought pattern: "I work hard, so I should treat myself."
- Behaviour: Overspending on things that give short-term happiness but long-term stress.
- Fix: Give yourself room for fun but build it into your budget—treating yourself shouldn't mean sabotaging your future.

3. The "I'll Figure It Out Later" Mindset

- Thought pattern: “I don’t have time to worry about money.”
- Behaviour: Ignoring bills, not saving, avoiding reality.
- Fix: Set small, manageable financial goals so you can take control without feeling overwhelmed.

First Step: Identify Your Money Mindset

Take a moment to reflect:

1. What are your earliest memories about money?
2. What messages did you learn about money growing up?
3. How do you currently feel when you check your bank account?

Write these answers down somewhere. The more self-aware you become about your financial habits, the easier it will be to change them.

Next Steps: Using Your Budget Tracker to See Where Your Money Goes

Now that you’ve started thinking about your money mindset, it’s time to get real about your finances.

- Download and open the **Break Free Budget Tracker.** (Information on how to purchase on page 56)
- List all your income sources (salary, side hustles, benefits, etc.).

- Write down every expense you have—rent, bills, food, subscriptions, and even small daily spending.
- Open all those letters and write down all your debts (credit cards, loans, any bill arrears, etc.)(Use Debt Snapshot sheet page 70)
- Take a deep breath. This isn't about judgment; it's about understanding.

We'll use this information in the next chapter to break the paycheck-to-paycheck cycle for good.

CHAPTER 2: BREAKING THE PAYCHECK-TO-PAYCHECK CYCLE

Why We Stay Stuck in Financial Struggles

The paycheck-to-paycheck cycle is exhausting. You get paid, cover your bills, maybe treat yourself a little because "you deserve it," and then—before you know it—you're back to counting down the days until payday.

I know this cycle well because I lived it. No matter how much I earned, I always felt like I was struggling. I wasn't living beyond my means in a flashy way, but I wasn't managing my money either.

What kept me stuck? Shame, avoidance, and comparison.

Tina's Story: The Weight of Avoidance

"I remember the first time I ignored a letter from a creditor. It felt easier to push it aside than to face the reality of my situation. But that one letter turned into two, then five, then a pile I refused to open. Each time I saw an envelope with a creditor's name on it, my stomach dropped. Instead of dealing with the problem, I hid from it—literally. I stuffed letters in drawers, convinced myself I'd "sort it out later," and told myself that everyone else was doing fine except me."

The thing is, ignoring financial problems doesn't make them go away—it makes them worse. Interest kept piling up, the debt gets bigger, and the stress of avoiding it consumed you. Being afraid of judgment will stop you from reaching out for help.

But here's what you can learn: creditors want their money. They would much rather work with you on a manageable payment plan than have you disappear. The minute you opened those letters, called the creditors, and explained your situation, things will start shifting.

Step 1: Face Your Financial Reality Without Shame

The first step to breaking the paycheck-to-paycheck cycle is facing the truth. Not with judgment, not with guilt—but with clarity.

- Open every financial letter and email you've been avoiding.
- Write down all your debts, balances, and minimum payments. (Use the Debt Snapshot Sheet on page 70)
- Be honest about where your money is going each month.

❢ **Psychology Tip:** Money shame keeps people stuck. Instead of beating yourself up, remind yourself: "I am not my debt. I am taking control."

Mastering Debt Communication: The Power of Creditor Letters/Emails

One of the most important steps in regaining financial control is effectively communicating with your creditors. Ignoring letters and overdue notices only worsens the situation, but a well-crafted letter can help you freeze interest, negotiate payment plans, or even request debt reductions.

In this book we will detail where you'll be able to have access to a collection of powerful creditor letter/email templates designed to help you take charge of your debt. These include:

- Request to Freeze Interest & Charges – To stop debts from spiralling while you get back on track.
- Affordable Payment Plan Proposal – To set up a realistic and manageable repayment schedule.
- Financial Hardship Letter – If you're struggling due to unforeseen circumstances, this letter helps explain your situation and seek leniency.
- Debt Settlement Request – For negotiating a reduced lump-sum payment.

These letters/emails are not just templates, they are tools to empower you to face your debt head-on. Paired with the strategies in this book, they will help you regain control, reduce stress, and start moving toward financial freedom.

Step 2: Set Up a Simple Budget That Works for You

The word "Budget" used to make me cringe. It felt restrictive, like I'd have to live a boring, joyless life. But I soon realised that a budget isn't about restricting you—it's about freeing you. When you have control over your money, you stop stressing about it.

How to Use Your Break Free Budget Tracker

- Prioritise essential expenses first. Rent/mortgage, food, utilities, and minimum debt payments come first.
- Identify areas to cut back on. Are there subscriptions you don't use? Can you switch to a cheaper phone plan? Small tweaks add up.

Step 3: Create a Manageable Debt Repayment Plan

If your debt payments are too high and eating up most of your paycheck, renegotiating your repayment terms can help. Using the correct letter template will help you build confidence in communicating with your creditors.

The Paycheck Trap: Why You Always Feel Broke

I used to wonder: "Why am I always broke, even when I earn more?"

It felt like no matter how hard I worked; I was always waiting for the next payday to feel secure. The cycle went like this:

→ Get paid → Pay bills → Buy essentials → Try to enjoy life → Run out of money before payday → Repeat.

Sound familiar?

The problem wasn't how much I was earning, it was how I was managing my money. Breaking free from the paycheck-to-paycheck cycle isn't about cutting out all fun, it's about having a system that works for you.

Step 1: Create a One-Month Financial Buffer

The first step to breaking the cycle is building a cushion so you're not living paycheck to paycheck.

💡 **Goal: Save at least one month's worth of expenses.**

This means that instead of relying on next month's paycheck to cover this month's bills, you're always a month ahead.

How to Build Your One-Month Buffer (Even If Money is Tight)

✓ Cut Non-Essentials for 1-2 Months A short-term sacrifice for long-term relief.
✓ Use 'Extra' Money – Tax refunds, bonuses, or side gig earnings go straight into savings.
✓ Start Small – If one month's expenses is too much, aim for 1-2 weeks' worth first.

Once you have this buffer, you'll stop feeling like you're always running out of money.

Step 2: Pay Yourself First (The System That Works)

Most people spend first and save what's left. The problem? There's usually nothing left.

The key to financial freedom is paying yourself first.

✓ As soon as you get paid, put money into savings and essentials first.
✓ Then, budget for everything else.

❢ **Example:**

If you earn £2,000 per month, before spending anything, you could:

✓ Save £200

✓ Pay off an extra £100 of debt

✓ Put £50 toward an emergency fund

Now, you're making progress before spending on anything else.

Step 3: Increase Your Income (Without Burnout)

If you've cut all unnecessary expenses but still feel stuck, it might be time to increase your income.

Ways to Make More Money (That Won't Take Over Your Life)

1. **Ask for a Raise** – If you've been in your job for a while, prepare a case and negotiate.
2. **Freelancing or Side Hustles** – Selling skills online (writing, graphic design, tutoring, etc.).
3. **Selling Unused Items** – Clothes, electronics, and furniture can bring in extra cash.
4, **Monetising a Hobby** – Do you bake, paint, or create content? Turn it into extra income.

Increasing your income doesn't mean working yourself to exhaustion, it means finding smarter ways to earn.

Step 4: Plan for the Future (So You Never Struggle Again)

❢ **The key to long-term financial security? A solid plan.**

✓ Emergency Fund: Continue saving until you have 3-6 months of expenses.
✓ Debt Freedom: Focus on clearing high-interest debts first.
✓ Investing: Start small—just £50 a month can grow into thousands over time.
✓ Passive Income: Look into long-term income streams that can earn you money without using huge amount of your time

❢ **Psychology Tip:** If you feel embarrassed about contacting creditors, remember they deal with financial hardship cases every day. You're not alone, and they would rather help you pay off your debt than have you default.

Progress Over Perfection

Breaking the paycheck-to-paycheck cycle doesn't happen overnight. It's about small, consistent steps. The key is to start.

✓ Face your financial reality. No more avoiding letters.
✓ Create a budget that works for YOU.
✓ Talk to your creditors. Negotiate a plan that won't leave you broke.
✓ Remind yourself: You are not your debt. You are taking control.

CHAPTER 3: CREATING A BUDGET THAT WORKS FOR YOU

Why Most Budgets Fail (And How Yours Won't)

If you've ever tried to budget before and failed, you're not alone.

I remember my first attempt at budgeting. I wrote out all my expenses, promised myself I'd cut back, and felt confident. But within a few weeks, I had completely abandoned it. **Why?** Because I made the same mistakes most people do:

❌ **I made my budget too restrictive.** I cut out everything "unnecessary," which made life miserable.
❌ **I didn't track my spending.** I assumed I was sticking to my budget, but small daily purchases added up.
❌ **I had no flexibility.** If an unexpected expense popped up, my whole budget collapsed.

Sound familiar? Budgeting only works if it's realistic, flexible, and built around your actual life.

Step 1: Find Your Starting Point

Before you can create a budget, you need to understand where your money is actually going. This is the part most people avoid, but trust me, knowledge is power.

For the next 7-14 days, write down every single expense. Yes, even the £3 coffee. The goal is to see patterns in your spending so you can make changes without feeling deprived.

✓ Use the **Weekly Spending Tracker** to log your spending (page 63)
✓ Categorise expenses: rent, food, bills, transport, debt payments, savings, entertainment, etc.
✓ Be honest. No judgment— it's just data.

Step 2: Build a Budget That Fits Your Life

Once you know where your money is going, it's time to give every pound a purpose. Here's a simple budgeting formula that works for most people:

The 50/30/20 Rule
→ 50% - Needs (Rent, bills, food, transport, debt payments)
→ 30% - Wants (Eating out, entertainment, hobbies, subscriptions)
→ 20% - Savings & Debt Repayment

Example Budget #1: Single Person Earning £2,000/Month

- Needs (50%) = £1,000 (rent, bills, food, transport)
- Wants (30%) = £600 (gym, Netflix, eating out, fun money)

- Savings & Debt (20%) = £400 (savings & extra debt payments)

Example Budget #2: Parent Earning £2,500/Month

- Needs (50%) = £1,250 (rent/mortgage, utilities, food, childcare, transport)
- Wants (30%) = £750 (kids' activities, eating out, fun money)
- Savings & Debt (20%) = £500 (savings & paying off debt faster)

Understand that in certain situations, you will need to reduce you "Wants" percentage to compensate for your higher "Needs" cost. When this happens, take a moment to reflect on your expenses, "Am I just trying to keep up with everyone else", rather than live within your means. The goal is to stick as closely to this ratio as possible, giving you more financial freedom and less stress.

Step 3: Make Your Budget Work in Real Life

A budget isn't just numbers on a page. It should work for you, not against you.

Budgeting Tips to Stay on Track

✓ Give yourself fun money. If your budget is too strict, you'll give up. Allow yourself a small "guilt-free" spending amount.
✓ Plan for the unexpected. Set aside a little each month for surprise expenses (car repairs, medical bills, etc.).
✓ Use cash for problem areas. Struggle with overspending? Withdraw a set amount in cash for things like groceries or

entertainment. Once it's gone, it's gone.

✓ Adjust as needed. Your budget should change with your life. Don't feel guilty about adjusting categories if needed.

Step 4: Make Room for Debt Repayment

If you're in debt, part of your budget needs to go toward paying it off in a way that doesn't leave you broke.

💡 **Psychology Tip:** The key is to stay consistent. It's better to pay £50 a month for a year than to overcommit to £200 and quit after two months.

How to Prioritise Your Debt Payments

1. **Cover the minimum payments on all debts first.** This keeps your accounts in good standing.

2. **Decide on a debt strategy:**

- **The Snowball Method**: Pay off the smallest debt first for quick wins.
- **The Avalanche Method**: Pay off the highest-interest debt first to save money long-term.

3.**Negotiate if needed.** If your minimum payments are too high, ask your creditors for a lower, more manageable plan.

<u>Progress Over Perfection</u>

💡 **Motivation Reminder:** You don't need to be perfect, you just need to be consistent.

✓ A budget is a tool, not a punishment.

✓ You don't have to cut out everything you enjoy—just

spend intentionally.

✓ Your past mistakes don't define your future. What matters is what you do next.

CHAPTER 4: MANAGING DEBT WITHOUT STRESS

Debt Doesn't Define You—It's Just a Problem to Solve

Debt can feel overwhelming. It weighs on your mind, keeps you up at night, and makes you feel like you're constantly drowning. But here's the truth:

→ Debt is just a math problem. It's numbers on a page, not a measure of your worth.
→ You are not alone. Millions of people struggle with debt, but many have overcome it, and so will you.
→ Small steps create big changes. No matter how much you owe, you can get through this one step at a time.

I know what it's like to feel ashamed of debt and avoid dealing with it. I used to ignore letters from creditors, hoping the problem would magically go away. It didn't. Instead, my balances got bigger, my stress got worse, and I felt completely stuck.

Everything changed when I finally stopped running and faced my finances head-on. That's when I realised: there is always a way forward.

Step 1: Get a Clear Picture of Your Debt

Before you can take control of your debt, you need to see the full picture.

❢ **Action Step:** Write down ALL your debts, including:
✓ Who you owe (credit cards, loans, overdrafts, payday loans, etc.)
✓ How much you owe
✓ Interest rates
✓ Minimum monthly payments

If you're using the **Break Free Budget Tracker**, there's a section specifically for tracking debts. Seeing everything in one place is powerful, start by writing down all debts on the **Debt Snapshot Sheet** (page 70), it turns the unknown into something you can tackle.

Step 2: Choose a Debt Payoff Strategy

Once you know what you owe, it's time to create a plan that works for YOU.

Debt Repayment Methods

1. **The Snowball Method** – Pay off the smallest debt first for quick wins.
2. **The Avalanche Method** – Pay off the highest-interest debt first to save money.
3. **Hybrid Approach** – A mix of both: Pay off small debts for motivation while tackling high-interest ones strategically.

❗ Example:

- If you owe £300 on a store card (19% interest) and £2,000 on a credit card (29% interest), the Avalanche Method would target the credit card first (to save money on interest), while the Snowball Method would target the store card first, to get a psychological boost.

Choose the method that keeps you motivated and fits your budget.

Step 3: Reduce Your Monthly Debt Payments

If your debt repayments are too high, don't panic, you can renegotiate. Creditors prefer receiving smaller payments than nothing at all.

❗ **Psychology Tip:** Many people avoid calling creditors because they fear judgment or rejection. But remember, this is just business for them. They aren't emotionally invested in your debt like you are.

How to Negotiate with Creditors

✓ Ask for a lower monthly payment.

✓ Request a temporary freeze on interest.

✓ See if they will remove late fees.

✓ Offer a repayment plan that actually works for you.

If they refuse your offer, don't give up. Keep negotiating or seek help from free third-party companies like *StepChange - a free debt advice service* that can advocate on your behalf.

Step 4: Avoid Common Debt Traps

To stop debt from growing, you need to avoid these common pitfalls:

✕**Making only minimum payments.** This keeps you trapped in debt for years. Even a little extra each month makes a difference.

✕ **Borrowing to pay off debt.** Avoid payday loans or using one credit card to pay another. It only makes things worse.

✕ **Ignoring bills.** Missed payments hurt your credit score and increase interest charges. Always contact creditors before missing a payment.

✕ **Thinking debt is normal.** Just because debt is common doesn't mean it should be permanent. You deserve financial freedom.

Step 5: Stay Motivated & Keep Going

Paying off debt is a journey, and it's easy to feel discouraged. But every step forward, no matter how small, is progress.

Motivation Boost: Imagine Your Life Debt-Free

→ No more stress when you check your bank account.

→ No more avoiding calls from unknown numbers.

→ More freedom to save, invest, and enjoy life.

💡 **Psychology Tip:** The key to staying motivated is celebrating small wins. Paid off a credit card? That's a victory. Stuck to your budget for a month? That's progress.

Your debt doesn't have to control you. You are taking control.

Chapter 5:
Building Better Spending Habits

Money isn't just about numbers, it's deeply tied to our emotions, habits, and past experiences. If you've ever wondered "Where did all my money go?" or found yourself spending impulsively even when you know you shouldn't, you're not alone. The good news? You can change your spending habits and take back control of your finances without feeling deprived.

This chapter will guide you through:

✓ Understanding why you spend the way you do

✓ Identifying bad spending habits and replacing them with better ones

✓ Learning practical strategies to make smarter financial choices

✓ Building a mindset that supports long-term financial stability

1. Why We Overspend: The Psychology Behind It

Spending is often emotional, not logical. Many of us were never taught how to manage money, and instead, we develop spending patterns based on our upbringing, social influences, and emotional needs.

Here are some common reasons people overspend:

- **Emotional Spending:** Buying things to cope with stress, sadness, or boredom.
- **Lifestyle Creep:** Increasing spending as income rises, rather than saving or investing.
- **Social Pressure:** Feeling the need to keep up with others (even if they're also struggling financially).
- **Impulse Purchases:** Making unplanned buys due to sales, advertising, or convenience.
- **Lack of Awareness:** Not tracking expenses, leading to "accidental" overspending.

2. Identifying Your Spending Triggers

The first step to changing your spending habits is recognising what triggers you to spend unnecessarily. Ask yourself:

- When do I spend money the most? (e.g., online shopping at night, after a stressful day)
- What emotions drive my spending? (e.g., happiness, anxiety, boredom)
- Are there certain places or people that influence my spending?
- Do I buy things on credit, even when I don't need to?

Once you pinpoint your triggers, you can find healthier alternatives to deal with them. Instead of impulse shopping when stressed, try going for a walk, journaling, or calling a friend.

3. The Power of Conscious Spending

Better spending habits don't mean cutting out everything you enjoy, it's about spending with purpose. Instead of asking, "Can I afford this?", ask:

✓ "Does this purchase align with my financial goals?"

✓ "Will this matter to me in a month?"

✓ "Is this a want or a need?"

Practical Steps to Spend Smarter:

✓ **Use the 24-Hour Rule:** If you see something you want, wait 24 hours before buying. This helps reduce impulse purchases.

✓ **Create a Budget for Fun Spending:** Allow yourself a set amount each month for guilt-free treats, so you don't feel deprived.

✓ **Unsubscribe from Temptation:** Remove yourself from promotional emails, sales alerts, and online shopping apps.

✓ **Use Cash or a Debit Card:** If credit cards tempt you to overspend, try using cash for discretionary spending.

✓ **Track Every Pound:** Use a spending tracker to see where your money is actually going—it's eye-opening!

4. The Mindset Shift: From Spending to Investing in Your Future

Instead of thinking of money as something to spend, start seeing it as a tool for freedom and security. Every pound you save or invest is working toward your future, reducing financial stress, and giving you more options in life.

New Mindset vs. Old Mindset:

Old Spending Mindset	New Smart Money Mindset
"I deserve this, I'll figure it out later."	"I deserve financial peace."
"It's on sale, so I have to buy it."	"A discount doesn't mean I need it."
"I'll start saving when I earn more."	"I can start managing my money right now."
"I need to keep up with everyone else."	"My financial goals matter more than appearances."

5. Setting Yourself Up for Success

Changing your spending habits takes time, but small, consistent changes add up.

Action Steps:

- **Set a Clear Financial Goal** – Whether it's paying off debt, saving for a home, or building an emergency fund, knowing why you want to improve your spending will keep you motivated.
- **Create a Spending Plan** – Instead of a restrictive budget, plan how much you'll spend in different areas (essentials, savings, fun money).
- **Find an Accountability Partner** – Share your goals with someone who will support you in making better money choices.

- **Review Your Progress Weekly** – Choose a day each week to sit and asses how your finances have been tracking. Reflect on your wins, learn from slip-ups, and keep improving.

Spend with Purpose

Money should work for you, not control you. By building better spending habits, you'll feel more in control, less stressed, and more empowered to create the life you truly want, without financial regret.

Start today. Track your spending for one week using the **Weekly Spending Tracker** (page 63) and notice where your money goes. Awareness is the first step to transformation.

CHAPTER 6:
SAVING MONEY WHILE STILL ENJOYING LIFE

"I Can't Afford to Save" (The Mindset Shift You Need)

For years, I told myself I couldn't afford to save.

I thought, "I'll start saving when I earn more."

But when I got a raise, I still didn't save.

Then I thought, "I'll save when I'm debt-free."

But even as my debt shrank, I wasn't building savings.

That's when I realised: Saving isn't about how much you earn—it's about what you do with what you have.

No matter your income, you can start saving now, even if it's just £5 a month. The key is making saving a habit, not an afterthought.

Step 1: Build an Emergency Fund (Even If You Have Debt)

An emergency fund is your financial safety net. It stops unexpected expenses from throwing you back into debt.

How Much Should You Save?

✓ **Goal #1: £500-£1,000** – Enough to cover small emergencies (car repairs, unexpected bills, etc.).
✓ **Goal #2: 3-6 months of expenses** – For long-term security.

💡 **Psychology Tip:** Big savings goals feel overwhelming. Instead, focus on saving one month of expenses at a time.

How to Save an Emergency Fund (Even on a Tight Budget)

1. **Automate It.** Set up a direct debit to a separate savings account. Even £10 a week adds up.
2. **Use 'Found Money.'** Tax refunds, work bonuses, or cashback rewards. Put them straight into savings.
3. **Sell Unused Items.** Old clothes, electronics, or furniture. Sell them and add the cash to your emergency fund.
4. **Cut Small Expenses (Without Feeling It).** Example:

- **Switching energy providers** = £20/month saved
- **Canceling unused subscriptions** = £10/month saved
- **Making lunch at home twice a week** = £30/month saved

These amounts can be combined and go towards your savings each month.

Step 2: Save Without Feeling Deprived

Most people think saving means giving up everything fun. But saving isn't about sacrificing your happiness, it's about spending smarter.

How to Save Money Without Feeling It

✓ Try the 'One-Month Rule.' Want to buy something expensive? Wait 30 days. If you still want it, then buy it.
✓ Have 'No-Spend Weekends.' Challenge yourself to spend £0 on entertainment for one weekend a month.
✓ Use the 50/30/20 Rule: (From Chapter 3) – 50% needs, 30% wants, 20% savings/debt.

Even with debt, you can split the 20% into both debt payments and savings:

✓ £300 to debt payments
✓ £100 to savings

Even a small savings habit builds financial security.

Step 3: Use Smart Saving Hacks

Want to save more without thinking about it? Try these:

✓ The 'Pay Yourself First' Trick – Transfer savings as soon as you get paid.
✓ Round-Up Savings Apps – Apps that have round up feature when making purchases and save the spare change.
✓ Cash-Only for Fun Spending – Withdraw cash for entertainment—when it's gone, it's gone.
✓ Meal Plan to Cut Food Costs – Planning meals reduces food waste and impulse takeaways.
✓ Use 'Sinking Funds' – Save a little each month for things like Christmas, holidays, or car repairs.

Step 4: Saving While Still Enjoying Life

💡 You don't have to give up fun—you just have to plan for it.

Example:

➡ Instead of eating out 4x a month £200, try eating out 2x and saving £100.

➡ Instead of buying coffee daily £80/month, try twice a week and save £50.

➡ Instead of impulse shopping £75, try putting £40 into savings first.

Small changes = big savings over time.

CHAPTER 7:
SMART SPENDING—HOW TO ENJOY LIFE WITHOUT WASTING MONEY

Spending Without Guilt: The Balance Between Fun and Finance

One of the biggest mistakes people make when fixing their finances is going too extreme.

I used to think the only way to save money was to cut out everything fun, no eating out, no trips, no treats. But that just made me miserable, and eventually, I gave up and overspent again.

The truth is, you can enjoy life while still managing your money wisely. It's all about making intentional choices.

The goal isn't to stop spending, it's to stop wasting.

Step 1: Identify Your "Happy Spending"

Instead of cutting everything, figure out what truly brings you joy.

💡 **Ask yourself:**

- What purchases bring me lasting happiness?

- What do I spend on that I regret later?
- Where can I cut back without feeling deprived?

Example: Two People, Two Different Priorities

➞ Person A loves travel but doesn't care about expensive clothes. They cut shopping costs but budget for trips.
➞ Person B loves fashion but prefers simple holidays. They cut back on travel but save for quality clothing.

Both people enjoy life—just in different ways. The key is knowing what matters most to YOU.

Step 2: Cut Costs Without Feeling It

Now that you know what matters, let's cut the expenses that don't.

Everyday Money-Saving Hacks

✓ **Shop Smarter:**

- Use cashback apps like TopCashback or Honey to save on online purchases.
- Buy second-hand for high-quality clothes, furniture, or electronics.
- Wait for sales or use discount codes instead of impulse-buying.

✓ **Reduce Food Costs:**

- Meal plan to avoid wasting money on takeaways.
- Buy in bulk and freeze leftovers.

- Try supermarket own-brand items (often the same quality for less).

✓ **Lower Monthly Bills:**

- Switch energy providers for a better rate.
- Cancel unused subscriptions (check bank statements for forgotten ones!).
- Call providers and negotiate deals for your phone, internet, or insurance.

✓ **Travel for Less:**

- Use flight comparison sites like Skyscanner to find cheap tickets.
- Travel off-peak or mid-week for lower prices.
- Book accommodation with kitchens to save on eating out.

Step 3: The "Fun Money" Rule

💡 You don't have to feel guilty for spending—just plan for it.

The Fun Money Budget

✓ 50/30/20 Rule: (From Chapter 3) – 30% is for wants.
✓ Set a Monthly "Guilt-Free" Spending Amount: E.g., £150 per month for personal treats.
✓ Use Cash or a Separate Account: Withdraw cash for fun spending, when it's gone, it's gone!

💡 **Real-Life Example:**

Emma used to spend £250 a month on impulse shopping but didn't feel any happier. She switched to a £100 "fun money" budget and used the extra £150 to save for a holiday. She still enjoyed treats, but now had something bigger to look forward to.

Step 4: Avoid Overspending Traps

Even smart spenders can fall into marketing tricks that make us waste money.

✓ Beware of "Buy Now, Pay Later" – It feels like free money but can lead to more debt.
✓ Avoid the "Just One More" Trap – Retailers use tricks to make you spend more (e.g., "Only 2 left!" or "Spend £50 for free shipping").
✓ Wait 24 Hours Before Big Purchases – This stops impulse buying.
✓ Unsubscribe from Store Emails – Fewer temptations = fewer unnecessary purchases.

CHAPTER 8:
PLANNING FOR A FINANCIALLY FREE FUTURE

Why Most People Stay Stuck (And How You Can Avoid It)

The biggest reason people struggle financially isn't lack of income, it's lack of direction.

Without a clear financial plan, you end up:
❌ Living paycheck to paycheck with no savings
❌ Stressed about money, even when earning more
❌ Making random financial decisions instead of intentional ones

💡 **The key to financial freedom isn't just spending less—it's knowing where you're going.**

Step 1: Define Your Financial Goals

Money without purpose gets wasted. That's why you need clear financial goals to stay motivated.

💡 **SMART Goal-Setting Formula:**

✔ Specific: What exactly do you want to achieve? (e.g., "Save £5,000 for a home deposit")

✓ Measurable: How will you track progress? (e.g., "Save £500 per month")
✓ Achievable: Is it realistic? (e.g., If you can only save £200 per month, adjust the timeline.)
✓ Relevant: Does this goal align with your values? (e.g., "I want to be debt-free so I can start my own business")
✓ Time-Bound: Set a deadline (e.g., "I'll save £5,000 within 12 months").

Examples of Financial Goals:

✓ Pay off £3,000 of my debt within 18 months
✓ Save a 3-month emergency fund (£6,000) in 2 years
✓ Invest £100 per month for long-term wealth

💡 **Write down your top 3 financial goals right now…**

Step 2: Create Your Long-Term Financial Plan

Now that you have goals, it's time to build a roadmap.

The 5-Step Financial Freedom Plan:

1. **Build an Emergency Fund** – Start with £500, then aim for 3-6 months' expenses.
2. **Pay Off High-Interest Debt** – Credit cards, loans—clear them before saving more.
3. **Increase Your Income** – Side hustles, promotions, or passive income sources.
4. **Save for Big Goals** – A home, travel, education, or early retirement.
5. **Invest for the Future** – Stocks, pensions, property—build long-term wealth.

❢ **You don't have to do it all at once. Start with Step 1 and 2 then work your way up.**

Step 3: Automate Your Wealth-Building

The easiest way to stay consistent? Automation.

✓ Set up automatic savings transfers – Treat savings like a bill.
✓ Use direct debits for debt repayment – No chance of forgetting.
✓ Invest automatically – Apps like Moneybox, Nutmeg, or Vanguard let you invest small amounts regularly. (Ensure you research before making any investments)

❢ **Real-Life Example:**

Sarah struggled to save money. She set up an automatic transfer of £50 every payday into a separate savings account. After a year, she had £600 without even thinking about it.

Step 4: Stay Motivated (Even When It Feels Slow)

Building wealth takes time, but consistency wins.

❢ **How to Stay Motivated:**

✓Create a vision board with all you financial goals, have it somewhere you will see every day.
✓ Track progress visually – Use a debt-payoff or savings tracker.
✓ Celebrate small wins – Every £100 saved or debt paid off is a step forward.
✓ Find a financial accountability partner – Someone to check

in with monthly.

✔ Remind yourself of WHY you're doing this – Financial freedom, less stress, and a better future.

Adopt a Long-Term Wealth Mindset

💡 **The habits that got you out of debt are the same habits that will make you wealthy.**

✔ Think long-term – Small daily financial choices add up over years.

✔ Surround yourself with people who inspire financial growth – Follow books, podcasts, and mentors.

✔ Keep learning and adjusting – Money management is a lifelong skill.

Chapter 9: Staying on Track & Avoiding Setbacks

Building better financial habits is one thing, sticking to them long-term is where the real challenge begins. Life happens. Unexpected expenses pop up, motivation fades, and old habits try to creep back in. But setbacks don't mean failure. The key to financial success isn't perfection; it's persistence.

This chapter will guide you through:

✓ Recognising common financial setbacks and how to handle them

✓ How to stay motivated when progress feels slow

✓ Strategies to bounce back quickly if you slip up

✓ How to make financial habits second nature

1. Expect Setbacks—But Don't Let Them Define You

One of the biggest mistakes people make is thinking that a financial setback means they've failed completely. But just like with dieting, exercise, or any habit change, progress isn't always linear. The goal isn't to be perfect, it's to stay committed.

Common Setbacks & How to Overcome Them:

Setback	Why It Happens	How to Get Back on Track
Unexpected Expenses	Car repairs, medical bills, home emergencies	Have an emergency fund in place & adjust your budget instead of relying on credit
Impulse Spending	Emotional shopping, sales, peer pressure	Use the 24-hour rule before purchases, unsubscribe from marketing emails
Losing Motivation	Slow progress, feeling restricted	Remind yourself of your "why," track wins, and reward progress
Income Changes	Job loss, reduced hours, pay cuts	Rework your budget, cut back on non-essentials, and explore additional income streams
Falling Back Into Debt	Relying on credit for daily expenses	Reassess spending habits, adjust your debt payoff plan, and seek support if needed

The most important thing? When you stumble, don't quit, adjust and keep going.

2. Staying Motivated When Progress Feels Slow

Financial freedom is a marathon, not a sprint. Some months will be harder than others, but staying focused on your end goal is what matters most.

Ways to Keep Yourself Motivated:

✓ Track Your Progress: Seeing your debt go down or savings go up—even slowly—keeps you inspired.
✓ Celebrate Small Wins: Paid off a credit card? Stuck to your budget for a full month? Reward yourself (in a budget-friendly way).
✓ Visualise Your Future: Imagine how life will feel when you're debt-free and financially secure.
✓ Remind Yourself of Your Why: Whether it's stress-free living, buying a home, or having more freedom, keep that goal in focus. (Create a vision board)

When motivation dips, look back at how far you've come instead of how far you still have to go.

3. Making Good Financial Habits Stick

Long-term success comes from making smart money habits automatic. The less you have to think about them, the easier they are to maintain.

How to Make Financial Habits a Lifestyle:

✓ Automate Your Finances: Set up direct debits for bills, savings, and debt repayments so you never have to think about them.
✓ Check Your Finances Weekly: Spend 20-35 minutes

reviewing your spending and progress to stay on top of things.

✓ Keep Learning: Read financial books, listen to money podcasts, and keep growing your knowledge.

✓ Surround Yourself with Support: Follow people who inspire you, and avoid those who encourage bad spending habits.

✓ Adjust When Needed: Life changes, and so should your budget. Regularly tweak your plan to keep it realistic.

4. Bouncing Back from a Slip-Up

Let's be real, at some point, you're going to overspend, forget to budget, or take a financial hit. The trick is knowing how to recover without completely derailing your progress.

Steps to Get Back on Track:

1. Acknowledge it (Without Guilt): Accept that setbacks happen, it doesn't erase your progress.
2. Review what went wrong: Was it emotional spending? Poor planning? An emergency?
3. Adjust your budget: Shift things around for the next month to get back on track.
4. Make a plan to avoid it again: If impulse spending got you, put blockers in place (delete shopping apps, use cash instead of cards).
5. Refocus & Keep Going: A bad financial week or month doesn't mean failure—it's just a detour.

The only real mistake is giving up. Keep moving forward, even if it's one small step at a time.

Progress Over Perfection

Financial success isn't about never messing up, it's about getting back on track faster each time. Stay patient, stay committed, and remind yourself why you started.

Take control of your finances, stay focused, and keep pushing toward the financial freedom you deserve. Your future self will thank you.

Conclusion:
Your New Financial Life

You've made it to the end of this journey, but really, this is just the beginning. You now have the tools, strategies, and mindset to take control of your finances and create a life where money works for you, not against you.

Recap: The Key Steps to Financial Freedom

Throughout this book, we've worked through the foundations of building a better financial future. Whether you're just starting out or further along in your journey, these key steps will always apply:

✓ Face Your Finances Head-On – No more ignoring debt, overspending, or feeling ashamed. Awareness is the first step to change.

✓ Master Your Budget – Track your income, expenses, and spending habits to stay in control.

✓ Tackle Your Debt – Use a structured plan to eliminate debt without overwhelming yourself.

✓ Build an Emergency Fund – Having savings prevents you from falling back into financial stress.

✓ Adopt Smart Spending Habits – Avoid impulse spending, make intentional purchases, and live within your means.

✓ Stay on Track & Overcome Setbacks – Progress isn't about perfection, it's about consistency and resilience.
✓ Plan for the Future – Once you've stabilised your finances, shift your focus to saving, investing, and growing your wealth.

Your financial freedom isn't a one-time achievement—it's a lifetime commitment to making better choices.

Creating a Sustainable Financial Routine

Financial success isn't about big, dramatic changes, it's about small, consistent actions that become second nature over time. The more automated and effortless your money habits are, the easier it will be to stay on track.

Daily Money Habits:

✓ Check Your Bank Balance – Stay aware of your spending and avoid surprises.
✓ Make Mindful Spending Decisions – Pause before making purchases. Ask: *Is this a need or a want?*
✓ Avoid Financial Triggers – Unsubscribe from marketing emails and avoid impulse spending temptations.

Weekly Money Check-Ins:

✓ Review Your Budget – Look at your spending and make adjustments where needed.
✓ Plan for Upcoming Expenses – Make sure you're prepared for bills, groceries, and any planned purchases.

Monthly Financial Goals:

✓ Make a Debt or Savings Payment – Even small amounts move you forward.

✓ Reflect on Your Progress – Celebrate wins and adjust your strategy where needed.

✓ Stay Educated – Read books, listen to finance podcasts, or follow money experts for continued learning.

Your routine should fit your lifestyle. The goal isn't restriction, it's financial confidence and security.

Encouragement & Next Steps

If you take one thing away from this book, let it be this: You have the power to change your financial future.

✓ You don't have to live in constant money stress.

✓ You don't have to feel trapped by debt.

✓ You don't have to struggle paycheck to paycheck.

No matter where you're starting from, small, consistent changes will transform your financial life. You've already taken the first step by educating yourself—now it's time to put these strategies into action.

💡 **Next Steps:**

➞ Use the **Break Free Budget Tracker** to keep your finances in check (Info on page 56)

➞ Take advantage of a free one-on-one consultation to set up your financial plan.

→ Stay accountable—share your goals with a trusted friend, partner, or financial coach.

The hardest part of any journey is taking the first step. You've done that. Now, it's about moving forward, one smart financial decision at a time.

Your future self is waiting. Go claim your financial freedom!

Your Personalised Financial Roadmap

Congratulations on taking this step toward financial control! Reading this book is a powerful move, but real transformation comes from taking action. You don't have to do it alone, here are some ways to keep going:

1. **Purchase Your Break-Free Budget Tracker**

To make tracking your finances easier, I've created a Five-Year Budget Tracker that will help you organise your spending, savings, and debt repayments.

This tool is designed to:

✓ Track your income, expenses, debt repayments, and savings goals over the next 5 years

✓ Give you a clear breakdown of where your money is going

✓ Help you stay consistent and avoid falling back into bad habits

✓ Adjust and update your financial plan as your life changes

Why 5 Years?

Most major financial goals, paying off debt, saving for a home, building an emergency fund, takes time. The tracker ensures you stay focused and motivated year after year.

As a reader of this book, you get exclusive offer for our **Break-Free Budget Tracker**, a tool designed to help you take control of your finances and stay on track, including all email templates. This is our way of helping you take action. Simply email contact@simones-solutions.com with the subject **'Tracker Access'** to claim yours today!

Your Free One-to-One Consultation

❢ Need help setting up your financial tracker?

With every Simone's Solution package, you'll get a free one-to-one coaching session where we:

✓ Go through your personal financial situation

✓ Set up your **Break-Free Budget tracker** to fit your lifestyle

✓ Create a plan that's realistic and achievable for you

✓ Answer any questions you have

💡 **Why This Matters:**

Most people struggle with money because they don't have a system. We'll make sure you start with a strong foundation.

📅 **Book your session today** – because the sooner you start, the sooner you see results. Contact us at: contact@simones-solutions.com

---

Free One-Month Check-In

Sticking to a new financial plan can be challenging, but you don't have to do it alone.

After your first session, we'll book and check in one month later to:

✓ Review your progress

✓ Adjust your budget if needed

✓ Help with any financial challenges you're facing

💡 This check-in ensures you stay on track and continue making progress toward your financial goals!

Letter Templates to Help You Contact Creditors

One of the hardest parts of dealing with debt is reaching out to creditors. To make this easier, we've included pre-written letter/email templates to help you:

✓ Ask for a lower monthly payment.
✓ Request a temporary freeze on interest.
✓ See if they will remove late fees.
✓ Offer a repayment plan that actually works for you.

💡 **Why This Matters:**

Many people avoid contacting creditors out of fear, but taking action puts you in control. Our templates help you communicate clearly and confidently.

Smart Money Moves, Extra Tips

Extra Money Tips to Accelerate Your Financial Journey

To help you go even further, here are some additional tips to maximise your financial success:

1. The 24-Hour Rule for Spending

Before making any non-essential purchase, wait **24 hours.**
✓ Helps you avoid impulse buying
✓ Gives you time to decide if it's truly necessary
✓ Saves you hundreds (or even thousands) over time

2. The £1 Per Use Rule

When buying something, ask: "Will I get £1 of value per use?"
✓ A £50 dress worn **50 times** = Good value
✓ A £100 gadget used **once** = Bad value

This rule helps you spend smarter on things that truly bring value.

3. Increase Your Income, Not Just Cut Expenses

Cutting expenses is great, but earning more accelerates your progress.
✓ Ask for a raise or promotion
✓ Start a side hustle (freelancing, tutoring, selling online)
✓ Monetise a skill you already have

💡 Even an extra £200/month can pay off debt or build savings faster.

4. Use the "Pay Yourself First" Method

Before spending on anything else, save or invest a portion of your income.
✓ Automate savings as soon as you get paid
✓ Treat savings like a non-negotiable bill
✓ Start small (even £20 per paycheck) and increase over time

💡 This method builds long-term wealth with minimal effort.

Free Financial Support Services: Get Help When You Need It

If you're struggling with debt, budgeting, or financial stress, you don't have to face it alone. These free financial services offer expert advice, debt solutions, and guidance to help you regain control of your finances.

1. Free Debt Advice & Management

- **StepChange (UK)** – Free, confidential debt advice and tailored solutions. (*www.stepchange.org*)
- **National Debtline (UK)** – Offers free support for managing debt and negotiating with creditors. (*www.nationaldebtline.org*)
- **MoneyHelper (UK)** – Government-backed financial advice and budgeting tools. (*www.moneyhelper.org.uk*)
- **Christians Against Poverty (CAP UK)** – Free debt help and budgeting support, open to everyone. (*www.capuk.org*)

2. Benefits & Financial Assistance

- **Citizens Advice (UK)** – Free guidance on benefits, budgeting, and legal rights. (*www.citizensadvice.org.uk*)
- **Turn2Us (UK)** – Helps people access grants, benefits, and financial aid. (*www.turn2us.org.uk*)

3. Mental Health & Money Support

- **Mind – Mental Health & Money Advice** – Practical financial help for those struggling with mental health issues. (*www.mentalhealthandmoneyadvice.org*)
- **Samaritans (UK)** – Free, confidential emotional support for those in distress. (*www.samaritans.org*)

4. Free Credit Score & Budgeting Tools

- **Experian, ClearScore & Credit Karma (UK)** – Free credit score checks and financial insights.

🌍 Global & Online Financial Assistance

- **Money Advice Service (Global)** – Offers financial guidance, budgeting tools, and debt management advice. (*www.moneyhelper.org.uk*)
- **United Way Worldwide** – Provides financial assistance programs and connects individuals with local resources. (*www.unitedway.org*)
- **Samaritans (International)** – Offers confidential emotional support for those in distress, including financial struggles. (*www.samaritans.org*)

Take the First Step to Financial Stability

If you're feeling overwhelmed by money worries, reach out for support. These services are completely free, non-judgmental, and designed to help you get back on track. You're not alone—help is available.

Weekly Spending Tracker: Know Where Your Money Goes

Why Tracking Your Spending Matters

One of the most powerful steps toward financial freedom is awareness. If you don't know where your money is going, it's easy to overspend, fall into debt, or miss opportunities to save. A weekly spending tracker helps you see your habits clearly, make adjustments, and take control of your financial future.

How to Use This Tracker

Each week, write down everything you spend money on, from big bills to small impulse buys. Be honest with yourself! At the end of the week, review your spending and reflect:

✓ Are you spending more than you earn?

✓ Are there unnecessary expenses you could cut?

✓ Did you stick to your budget?

✓ Are you prioritising your financial goals?

Analysing Your Spending

At the end of the week, total up your spending and ask yourself:

◆ Where did most of my money go?

- What purchases could I reduce or eliminate?
- Am I spending in alignment with my goals?

Challenge Yourself: The "No-Spend Day"

Try setting one day per week as a "No-Spend Day." This small habit can help you be more mindful of your money and break unnecessary spending habits.

Awareness Leads to Change

Tracking your spending is not about restriction, it's about empowerment. When you see where your money is going, you gain control, make better choices, and move closer to your financial goals.

Start today. Track your spending for a week and see what you discover!

Day	Category	Amount Spent	Was This Necessary? (Yes/No)	Notes/Reflection
Monday	*Example: Clothes*	*£45*	*No*	*New shoes for event/ I have plenty*
Tuesday				
Wednesday				
Thursday				
Friday				
Saturday				
Sunday				
Total				

Day	Category	Amount Spent	Was This Necessary? (Yes/No)	Notes/Reflection
Monday	*Example: Clothes*	*£45*	*No*	*New shoes for event/ I have plenty*
Tuesday				
Wednesday				
Thursday				
Friday				
Saturday				
Sunday				
Total				

Day	Category	Amount Spent	Was This Necessary? (Yes/No)	Notes/Reflection
Monday	*Example: Clothes*	*£45*	*No*	*New shoes for event/ I have plenty*
Tuesday				
Wednesday				
Thursday				
Friday				
Saturday				
Sunday				
Total				

Day	Category	Amount Spent	Was This Necessary? (Yes/No)	Notes/Reflection
Monday	*Example: Clothes*	*£45*	*No*	*New shoes for event/ I have plenty*
Tuesday				
Wednesday				
Thursday				
Friday				
Saturday				
Sunday				
Total				

Day	Category	Amount Spent	Was This Necessary? (Yes/No)	Notes/Reflection
Monday	*Example: Clothes*	*£45*	*No*	*New shoes for event/ I have plenty*
Tuesday				
Wednesday				
Thursday				
Friday				
Saturday				
Sunday				
Total				

Debt Snapshot Sheet: Get Clear on What You Owe

You Need a Debt Snapshot

Facing your debt head-on can feel overwhelming, but knowledge is power. The first step in taking control is understanding exactly what you owe. A Debt Snapshot Sheet helps you see all your debts in one place, making it easier to create a repayment plan, negotiate with creditors, and track your progress toward becoming debt-free.

How to Use This Sheet

Gather all your debt information, including loans, credit cards, overdrafts, and any money owed to individuals or companies. Fill in the table below, noting the total balance, interest rate, minimum payment, and due date for each debt.

How to Prioritise Your Debts

Not all debts are equal. Some need urgent attention to avoid penalties or legal action, while others can be paid off over time. Here's how to prioritise:

✓ High Priority – Debts with high interest rates, overdue payments, on the verge of legal action or essential bills (e.g., rent, utilities, tax debts).

✓ Medium Priority – Debts with manageable interest but that could grow over time (e.g., loans, credit cards).
✓ Low Priority – Low-interest debts or those with flexible payment terms.

What Comes Next?

Now that you have your debt snapshot, ask yourself:
◆ **Which debts should I pay off first?** (Consider starting with high-interest debt)
◆ **Can I negotiate a lower interest rate or set up a payment plan?**
◆ **Can I make extra payments on certain debts to reduce my total interest paid?**

Knowledge is Power

Seeing your debts written down can feel intimidating, but this is a step toward financial freedom. The more aware you are, the more control you have. Use this sheet to track progress, create a repayment strategy, and take charge of your financial future!

Debt Snapshot Sheet

Creditor/Lender	Total Balance	Interest Rate (%)	Minimum Payment	Due Date	Notes/Priority (High/Medium/Low)	Notes/Action Plan
Example: ABC Credit Card	*£2,500*	*24.9%*	*£75*	*15th of the month*	*High interest – Medium*	*Call to negotiate a lower interest rate (possibly increase monthly payment)*

Debt Snapshot Sheet

Creditor/Lender	Total Balance	Interest Rate (%)	Minimum Payment	Due Date	Notes/Priority (High/Medium/Low)	Notes/Action Plan
Example: ABC Credit Card	*£2,500*	*24.9%*	*£75*	*15th of the month*	*High interest – Medium*	*Call to negotiate a lower interest rate (possibly increase monthly payment)*

Debt Snapshot Sheet

Creditor/Lender	Total Balance	Interest Rate (%)	Minimum Payment	Due Date	Notes/Priority (High/Medium/Low)	Notes/Action Plan
Example: ABC Credit Card	*£2,500*	*24.9%*	*£75*	*15th of the month*	*High interest – Medium*	*Call to negotiate a lower interest rate (possibly increase monthly payment)*

Debt Snapshot Sheet

Creditor/Lender	Total Balance	Interest Rate (%)	Minimum Payment	Due Date	Notes/Priority (High/Medium/Low)	Notes/Action Plan
Example: ABC Credit Card	*£2,500*	*24.9%*	*£75*	*15th of the month*	*High interest – Medium*	*Call to negotiate a lower interest rate (possibly increase monthly payment)*

Debt Snapshot Sheet

Creditor/Lender	Total Balance	Interest Rate (%)	Minimum Payment	Due Date	Notes/Priority (High/Medium/Low)	Notes/Action Plan
Example: ABC Credit Card	*£2,500*	*24.9%*	*£75*	*15th of the month*	*High interest – Medium*	*Call to negotiate a lower interest rate (possibly increase monthly payment)*

Debt Snapshot Sheet

Creditor/Lender	Total Balance	Interest Rate (%)	Minimum Payment	Due Date	Notes/Priority (High/Medium/Low)	Notes/Action Plan
Example: ABC Credit Card	*£2,500*	*24.9%*	*£75*	*15th of the month*	*High interest – Medium*	*Call to negotiate a lower interest rate (possibly increase monthly payment)*

www.ingramcontent.com/pod-product-compliance
Lightning Source LLC
LaVergne TN
LVHW050922210926
848482LV00012B/505
* 9 7 8 1 0 3 6 9 3 0 1 8 9 *